Basic Executive Management Tips

Basic Executive Management Tips

Gaster Sharpley

Library of Congress Control Number: 2012909978
ISBN: Hardcover   978-1-4771-2259-4
                         Softcover   978-1-4771-2258-7
                         Ebook   978-1-4771-2260-0

First print, 2012

This book was printed by Harrys Printers, East London
Tel.: 043 703 8800 - www.harrysprinters.com

To order additional copies of this book, contact
Laurie Shaw Consulting
043 727 1070
www.laurieshaw.co.za
office@laurieshaw.co.za

Dedicated to Laurie Shaw

Contents

Acknowledgements

- Our Heavenly Father.

- Thanks to my colleagues for allowing me to coordinate complex decisions that required direction.

- Thank you to Faye Dolley for teaching me to use a computer.

- Once again thanks to my wonderful wife of twenty-four years.

- To Johnathan, thank you for the development I see in you.

- To Garth, let the world enjoy your golden personality.

- To Jazmine my grandchild, you are the light on a dark day.

GASTER SHARPLEY

Preface

Life has logical phases, and it is critical that you develop in the profession or area of focus with natural progression. Some of the phases may be shorter based on how quick you grasp the primary concepts that make up the phase. At some point you will develop sufficient skills and experience to become a manager and then an executive. This publication explores the basic issues of an executive manager and documents obvious issues that need to be considered. Most people wish to be in control and also enjoy the benefits of being the boss; however, very few are willing to take responsibility and make the necessary sacrifices required. The sacrifices must include a balance between the various aspects of life that will see you being a complete person rather than a complete executive and a lesser human being.

As you read this publication, you may from time to time feel that the information is basic and plain; however, you must consider it a reminder to take being an executive as a serious responsibility as at times it involves decisions about other people's lives. Being a successful executive is also made up of a range of issues coming together, including the people you work with, the people you choose to work with, your board, your clients, and your service providers. What am I saying? I am saying that you should not consider yourself a successful executive because of only who you are but because of who you are and the circumstances that you are in, more importantly, the people you surround yourself with. Enjoy the book.

Gaster Sharpley

GASTER SHARPLEY

I Am an Executive

What will I be when I grow old, something bold I am told

An executive may unfold

I am seven and my innocence belongs in heaven

The world becomes real and circumstances take away the thrill

At age sixteen, I take the stage and try to stay clean

Again I invoke the dream and am confused that it has attempted to defuse

I must keep a spark alight and keep putting up a brave fight

My world tells me to let go and go slow, but my desire remains on fire

As I up skill, possibilities I can feel

I can be an executive

I must maintain composure and build through sacrifice a composition that directs the scheme to revert to the dream

I start at the bottom so that I can appreciate reaching the top

Maturity, consistency, the right attitude – these are all attributes to lead me to my altitude

As I claim I must not tramp those I pass as my top will not last

I am an executive, I am on top but now I realise that the top is actually the bottom – as it is those at the bottom that keep you on top

Communicate, don't procrastinate, don't agitate as the time I have I must concentrate the focus on what I need to create

I am an executive

GASTER SHARPLEY

a. Boardroom Gangsters

> **He who puts up a fight could just be hiding his or her emotional plight.**

A gang is a group of people who have the same common goal of crime, easy money, and lavish lifestyles with very little effort put in. Members of the gang are referred to as gangsters. A gangster is best described as a person who has a criminal mind and seeks to devour all in his path in order to achieve money and a life of luxury using any means. There are classical examples of gangsters across the world depicted in Hollywood movies. This lifestyle seems inviting for the ambitious heart and offers quick reward for little work. Gangs have structured systems of governance, even if informal but it is easy to assess who the leader is and also the roles of the members based on their skills. The members are loyal and usually leave the gang only through death or imprisonment. Their dress code is predictable, with designer suits or popular name branded clothing with top-of-the-range sunglasses.

There seems to be a code of conduct for the members and informal rules that guide the relationship. Succession planning is predictable through the internship of younger recruits. The gangster will stop at nothing to reach his goal. At times this includes murder. Now, before this sounds romantic, it is still a life of crime and antisocial behaviour that remains a menace to a normal life. What about the boardroom? With the same motives of easy money and luxury lifestyles, it can be argued that there are gangsters in the corporate environment, the difference being that in the formal economy, the criminal mind is hidden by formal rules, guidelines, and fancy talk of making a difference. These are not gun-wielding or knife-carrying bad boys, but rather well-dressed gentlemen.

6. Going on an Executive Tangent with Boardroom Gangsters

Remember that even though you will find fault in others, you may be the fault to them.

A toxic environment infested with personal ambitions, greed, and power struggles is what the professional environment can turn out to be. Taking advantage of the volatile external environmental landscape and complex processes, the corridors are prowled by those seeking to gossip to mushroom an agenda that is not remotely associated with core business. On one extreme are the still powerful bunch from the bygone era dressed in new-age ideals of improving organisational performance and understand every fibre of boardroom bureaucracy. They use the system to maintain the control and manipulate the decision-making process by exploiting the ignorance of the passionate and compassionate shareholder. While this experience is needed and necessary, it has undermined the genuineness of transformation to grow organisations – a transformation that becomes necessary in the life of every company in order to remain relevant in a changing world.

Then there is the well-connected, well-meaning shareholder who is able to articulate the propaganda of change and reasonably qualified to hold a position in the administration of the organisation, but can't translate this into tangible outputs. This is caused by the constant attention being drawn to the game that has been carefully, yet unconsciously mastered of shifting the blame. Explanations there are, excuses plenty, time limited, but decay begins to creep into the system. It's okay as we can blame the past. The acquiring of a position of influence and authority removes the desire to learn and be mentored, leading to face value decisions and obvious conclusions rather than well – thought-through and permanent solutions for sustainable achievement of board resolutions. Let us not forget the naïve who come into the system to make a difference and base their approach on trust and openly share their thinking. To this humble soul the viscous, connive, and gently prey. The lack of understanding or refusal to understand how this informal system that is alive works leads the naïve head on into creating opportunities for the game. They are silenced by the subtle benefits such as travel and positions to subconsciously look the other way.

What about the one who struggled and was a great revolutionary for a better company as a worker but can't function in the deceit of the boardroom as he is focused on what he can get out? With a mind fixed on personal gain, he uses his executive position and control to exploit what is intended for the shareholder as he still considers himself as part of that definition. This leads to a path of destruction and careless outbursts that compromise even the most sober mind.

Many reduce what is happening to change, yet it's the same change in the whole company that instils opportunity and pain. It is the greedy that use the boardroom as a vehicle fuelled to create common camps and societies to outsmart each other to maintain or gain control. It is clear that those that are gone and those being targeted to go also played the game and kept the focus on the boardroom rather than on the interests of the shareholder that need attention. The game has always been there but just keeps getting rougher and the casualties more with the complexities. Has it become virtually impossible to make a simple decision without conspiracy theories being branded? Accusations and fingerpointing break even the best of men, and even the best of men break the finger that is pointing.

How will this viscous cycle end of evident gangster mentality that has become acceptable even in the formal boardroom? When will the game stop and change begin? The shareholder will wait no more as the emotion of union slogans is silenced by isolation from value gain. Shall the voice of the shareholder be heard or was it only the descendants of those who marched against the company in the past and those who added coal to the fires of the former bosses that have become the shareholders? Are they protecting their own interests?

What has gone wrong? Who is to blame? Why is it that when we need to make the wrong right, we tend to first place blame? The line between administration and boardroom oversight has over the years gradually been crossed in both directions. Even if it is for good reasons, it creates an unreasonable reality. There is confusion between authority and power. The camps have established foundations and battle lines are drawn too deep to turn back. Roles and responsibilities are not properly separated. Returns for the shareholder and core business have been relegated to a conversation. No one knows who owns the game as all become players even by refusing to play. There are more bosses and fewer technicians.

Let us hope that when the dust settles after a new term arrives for new board members and executive management, sanity will remove the emotions of alliances and the victorious shall look to the shareholder for a while before they become comfortable and repeat history again. It is not the logo that will help the shareholder grow. It is not charisma that will stop the child from weeping. Let there be a better life in this beautiful organisation. Let it give a voice to those who want to criticise having a workable solution. We must not give up and hope that the greedy will give up because of the determination of the shareholder. The gangster must be removed and core business must remain.

c. Back to Basics

Let the fundamentals move you and not your confidence.

Wow, at least I got that off my chest! The modern boardroom is complex and demands unique individuals who can navigate through the various challenges that face a CEO daily. Knowing the context of my tangent above that all it should be – context – and not a depressing approach to negative energy that it's all doom. Now that you know what you are dealing with in the workplace, you are able to be clear minded and determined to find your focus areas that will elevate the organisation. It is critical to also focus on building a team with those colleagues who are willing to and show the ability to work. In any workday, you should ensure that you create a balance in the issues that you deal with between those that are negative and critical in nature and those that are constructive. Be complimentary to your colleagues and don't bully them because you can achieve more through affirmation and recognition of the positive.

The approach of this publication is to consider the basics within Executive Management given the context of the environment and ever-changing environment. There are huge opportunities to make a considerable contribution and leave a legacy in the organisation you lead; however, you must be mindful of your surroundings and opportunities that may not be obvious to ordinary employees. Since being an executive holds a material benefit to personal comfort, the positions will always be contested. Let's now take the discussion to the ordinary daily debates to improve the workplace with a focus on strategic and operational considerations. As an executive, please know that your previous experience is only a point of reference and not a model because every environment is different.

d. I Want to Be an Executive Manager

Be prepared to take on the responsibility with the reward of being an Executive.

The decision to become an executive manager must be made against the backdrop of the tangent articulated above. Yes, it possesses negativity and startling realities of survival tactics adopted in boardrooms due to the complex nature and demanding pressure of the environment. I have selected to begin with this negativity as a result of our general approach to the achievement of an executive post. Let me explain. When applying for an executive post, the main areas of interest are as follows:

- **My career has moved up a notch or even two.**

- **I will make a difference.**

- **My lifestyle will improve.**

In the context of the dream to be appointed, we spend very little time thinking about the challenges that will emerge in the job. Now remember that there is nothing wrong with focusing on the good things, but do spare a thought of how you will navigate between the possible challenges in the context of knowing that with an understanding of the challenges, there is clarity of mind and better prospects of resolving issues. This harsh reality at times leads people to shy away from becoming executive managers and rather than focusing on the benefit of the job, the focus will be on the negative which includes,

- **I will be away from home a lot.**

- **I have to deal with other people's problems.**

- **I have to be working long hours.**

While the above it true, you need to restructure your life to merge other parts into the new job. You will be unproductive if you don't maintain a reasonable balance to your life. This balance includes spending time with family, church, hobbies, and other interests. Of course, as an executive you are expected to give priority to your job.

It can be argued that when you reduce the crisis issues in the workplace and put a system in place, you reduce the time you need to spend worrying about the workplace. It is critical that there is no clash between work and other activities – what I mean is that you should not carry your work into your bed, both physically and emotionally. It is unfair to seek advice from your spouse on matters that he or she may not be able to understand fully due to the lack of information regarding the complexities and dynamics that you experience before deducing that you have a problem.

In my view, this is precisely why executive placements should be contractual and short term. I further propose that you should take a break between executive jobs; however, this is achievable only if you are conservative with your income. So, this publication is about equipping the aspiring executive manager with relevant, yet basic information that will influence your behaviour in the work place by placing the issues in their context. The context I speak about is to separate strategic issues from operation matters. Strategic issues should also be further separated from governance related to executive management-related matters, while the operational issues should be separated into supervision of the implementation arm from actual delivery on core business. It is important to know your role/ responsibility/mandate/delegations and decision-making authority as an executive manager.

e. Context

Nothing happens in a vacuum and everything has a context that needs to be contextualised before action is taken.

The technological era and general freedoms in society have radically transformed management styles from an autocratic to a more liberal approach of consultation. Managers are expected to inspire rather than fire employees. The world over the modern manager can no longer be profiled as being 'white middle-aged male' but rather a basket of variations that suit either the organisation's desire to please the targeted market or one of many other factors that influence the boardroom debate on who should manage.

In the past, the focused criteria were age, gender, experience, and qualifications. The modern manager is appointed on other criteria such as appeal to the target market, out of the box thinking, radical, innovative, and a generalist on what is current. This new approach to select managers has relegated the other criteria to lesser importance.

It can also be said that the former version of managers focused on long-term growth and sustainability, and so they lost the immediate opportunities that may fall outside the organisation's systems mould. This also translated into the management positions being more long term or permanent. On the other hand, the modern manager looks for quick wins for fast growth informed by short-term contracts that pressurise the incumbent to deliver even if due process to measure sustainability is factored into the approach.

The past management style also allowed managers to consider all risks before making a decision and then taking full ownership of the resolution and its consequences, while the modern manager in most instances relies on the boardroom collective to make decisions. The democratisation of the boardroom can compromise accountability and decisive management and should be used as a think tank rather than as an operational decision-making body.

Let me not get ahead of myself and assume that the term manager is interpreted correctly for the sake of this publication. The graphic below illustrates the location of the manager, which is the subject of the book, in the context of an organisation. This structure is universal in character; however, there are various options of designing a company for functionality.

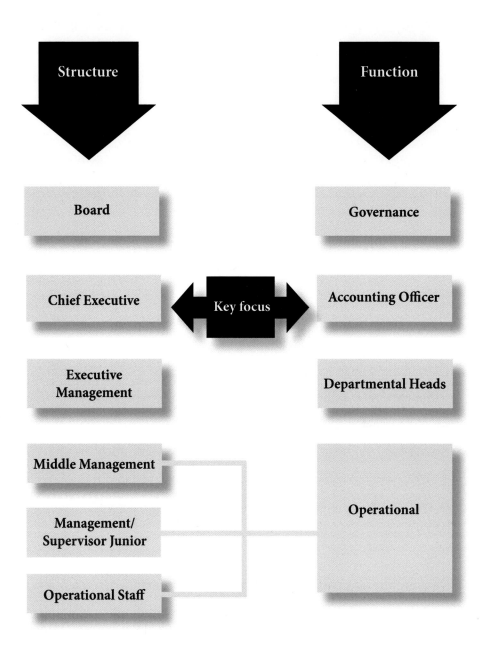

From the illustration, it can be understood that the target is the level of management that drives the organisation's activities. The skills base of the modern manager is expected to be generic and focused on project management rather than being based on past experience, which kept employees in a particular expertise for long years. As a reward of their many years of service, they become part of the management for their loyal service but it is the Accounting officer who makes all the decisions. The modern manager is appointed on what is termed merit; however, this sometimes deprives the company of a technical skill. Let me explain – school principals are appointed from a pool of educators, leaving a vacuum of the particular skill in the classroom. To add to this, let me refer you to another example – a top management post for a technical department will be advertised within a company, and the criteria would be to look for a person with the highest qualification in that particular skill. A functionary from the field or workplace would be selected and allowed to manage others. It is important that management skills should be accompanied by the technical ability; however, there should be a balance. A sound technician does not necessarily make a good manager and in turn, a good manager may not be a good leader on the governance structure.

What are the structures in a typical organisation?

- **Governance**

This structure is the supreme decision-making body that is usually tasked with the responsibilities of evolving strategies, overseeing tasked with the responsibilities of evolving strategies, overseeing operational functions, enumerating the budgeting, and employing senior management. The board is chaired by a chair or president and has between five and seven directors. The Chief Executive Officer (CEO) reports to the board. Due to pressure on organisations to remain relevant, there is a growing tendency to create a Managing Director (MD) in the place of a CEO. The MD serves on the board and runs the day-to-day operations of the organisation. The board makes decisions that are commonly known as resolutions that are then filtered into the operations of the company through the CEO. Organisational boards are usually structured as in the next diagram.

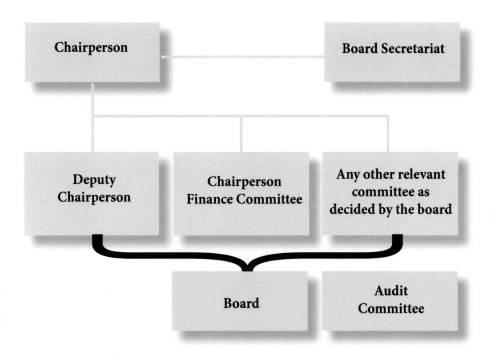

- **Management**

On the management side, the day-to-day operations of the company are run by layers of functionaries that implement the board resolutions. There is a growing trend to create flat structures – meaning that everyone is treated with mutual recognition for the function they serve. However, even in this instance, there is still a need for job titles and layers of responsibilities. The titles and responsibilities are normally governed by experience, qualifications, and passion. The operational structure is controlled by a CEO as the head, while a layer of top management serves as a point of reference for joint decision making. The top management usually comprises two distinct categories, namely, core business and support depending on the type of business. The following diagram shows a typical high-level structure in a company dealing with construction projects:

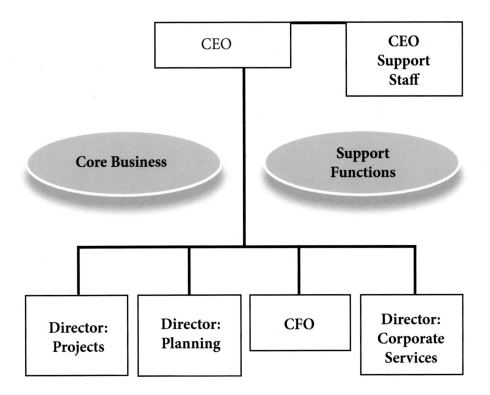

The modern company appoints top management on short-term contract between three and five years in order to maintain a high level of robust urgency to the vision. It can be argued that the best CEO is the one that governance board allows the space to run the operations based on agreed delegations and structured procedures. The King three report on good governance speaks in depth on the subject of the role of the board and the role of the CEO and management. The success of any company is in the calibre of the people it attracts and therefore this publication deals primarily with the attributes of a manager and offers advice of the key aspects of management. It is divided into two sections, namely, strategy and operations. This publication offers tips to heads of organisations (CEO, MD . . . etc.).

f. Strategy

> **You must picture the end in order to know where to start.**

1.   You got the job

The application process for a job is always clouded by anxiety, speculation, and anticipation. Many people want the job so badly that they pray for a job rather than praying for God's hand over their lives. It is important to know that most applicants pray and therefore, God is not going to get involved in the choosing game but leave that to the panel. However, God will allow the interview process to be one of the opportunities to display His love for you, whether you win or lose. Many people speculate what the panel would think and I have heard people say, 'It is not what you know but who you know.' After conversing with the promoter of this perception, it emerged that he was targeting a job that required a particular qualification (that he did not have) and relevant experience (that he had but in a different sector). What is the lesson? You may need to allow a professional recruitment agency to assess your personal profile and give you technically evaluated evidence of the jobs you can apply for. Job seeking should not be like taking lotto with a hope to win.

Given that all aspects of your profile are in place and you performed well in the interviews, there is the period when you must wait to hear whether you have the job or not. Some organisations decide quickly, while others take time. Oh, not to forget, for an executive management job, you will most likely be requested to do a competency assessment that evaluates you in three areas, namely, emotional state, competence, and the ability to apply logic and reason. Most organisations don't rely on the results to make a decision but rather use this information to assess the area in which you would require development.

Then the call comes, 'You got the job.' Take at least twenty-four hours to digest the call before reacting because the excitement may let you overlook certain valuable details that will be too late to manage once you commence duties. It is okay to be excited, but refrain from expecting a smooth journey in the job. There are a number of issues that require consideration before commencing duties, namely,

✔ **Personal issues** – What is the salary? What are the benefits? Now don't make any major financial decisions such as buying a new house or car until you have received at least three salaries and are able to evaluate the change in your lifestyle.

✔ **Professional issues** – Where is your new office? Who is your support staff such as a secretary? What is your decision-making powers and many other issues.

It is further important to leave your previous job on a good note and give the expected and appropriate notice rather than feeling pressurised to commence with the new job. Don't burn your bridges; the world is round and you will need to cross the bridge in the future even if the purpose of the bridge has changed. Let me unpack – your employer today could be your client tomorrow.

2.   On the first day

The first day in an office always reminds me of my first day of school. All my insecurities come in – I start questioning whether my decision to take the job was the correct one – I question whether I am able to meet the expectations of the new employer. Avoid making decisions on the first day and spend the day getting yourself familiar with the office and meeting your team. As a rule, I invite my family to my office for a few minutes for their own orientation of where I work since I discourage them visiting my office thereafter. Yes we love our families, but the workplace is a professional environment and it does not look good having children running up and down the passages while you are being remunerated to be productive and focused.

If you are the CEO, make sure that you speak to the Chairperson of the Board on day one with the intention of thanking the board again for the appointment. Never take your appointment for granted as it could be the result of extensive debate. Also ensure that the human resources department completes the formalities and all those compliance forms on the first day. You have no one to impress on day one and it is advisable to take lunch just to reflect halfway through the day. I usually invite my wife to lunch to discuss our long, healthy marriage and show her appreciation in an attempt to promise myself that I will be okay in the job.

Every company has informal practices and habits and any seasoned executive will be able to pick these up during the first few days. Some will be an irritation and the temptation will be there to go on the offensive and address the unnecessary issues; however, be careful of the complexities of organisational culture. You don't want your colleagues to comply out of pressure, but rather accept the significance for the need to change.

Use the first day to get to know your support staff such as the personal assistant. It is a good time to ask personal questions such as, 'Tell me about you.' This allows your employee to give you the information that he or she considers relevant. This will be the last time a personal question should come from you and this allows your employee to know that you care and that he or she can share personal achievements with you. There is obviously a balance that needs to be maintained as you don't find a job with the intention of finding friends.

3.   Understanding the organisation's vision

As the CEO it is important to understand and internalise the vision of the organisation. If there is no vision, craft one in consultation with your board and executive management. The vision is the road ahead for the company – a single statement that embodies the reason why the company exists. Many organisations appoint professionals to design the organisational market strategy and craft the vision. This might be fine; however, the vision is not about the English being used but should inform the reader of what the company is about and not focused on how eloquent the language is. One of the short comings in using the consultative method is that there could be a dominant stakeholder in the company who pushes the vision to represent their interest rather than speak about the organisation's need to communicate who and what it is about.

A vision must be accompanied by a mission – this is how the vision will be achieved, followed by objectives. Below is an example of a vision with a mission. This example is for a construction company that builds only office accommodation. The mission represents the 'how' part of the vision.

> **Vision: To be a market leader of quality office parks while empowering employees through social responsibility**

The vision above represents the elements of the now popular triple bottom line, which companies the world over have adopted;

✔ **Profit**

✔ **Environment**

✔ **Social responsibility**

Mission:

✔ **To understand the requirements of the client**

✔ **To adopt cutting-edge technologies to reduce costs and increase quality**

✔ **To develop the skills of employees in order to improve productivity**

✔ **To have a robust social responsibility that captures the desires of both management and staff.**

As the head of the company you must ensure that your team lives the vision, but avoid spending unnecessary time in meetings and workshops discussing the vision. Also, as the CEO, it is important to constantly reassure the board that the operations are linked to the vision and even the basics contribute to the bigger picture and road ahead for the organisation.

4. Identifying high-level excellence and challenges in employees

In any company, there are shining stars and passengers. You should be able to pick up who is able to deliver and who is able to just talk delivery. It is my belief that energy between people determines how they will respond to each other; therefore, it is important that if there is a negative energy with a colleague, then you find a way to work with the colleague to bring out the best in him or her, overshadowing the lack of energy between you both. Excellence should be measured in deliverables directly linked to the individual's responsibilities and also in the contribution they make to the big picture.

There is always the temptation to overload a willing colleague who delivers. Performing colleagues must be rewarded even in small ways, such as showing appreciation for what they do. Of course there are people who only do things to get recognition and who pretend to be the only one performing and as the CEO, you should refrain from satisfying this need for acknowledgement when it is not warranted.

On the other hand, there are employees who are just in over their heads. The main challenge with such employees is that some will pretend to know what they are doing and therefore hold the company back by fighting for survival rather than delivering on the mandate or tasks. In the case where an employee is aware that he or she does not meet the expected outputs assigned to him or her and admits this situation, you are able to assist him or her to develop. As the CEO, it is important for you to manage the company and not police it – what I mean is that there are some managers whose day is consumed by chasing subordinates while missing targets and blaming everyone else. Let the line managers address disciplinary issues with the corporate services section and keep the focus on those who want to assist you in achieving the goals. There are several steps that should be taken in addressing unproductive employees as illustrated in the next figure.

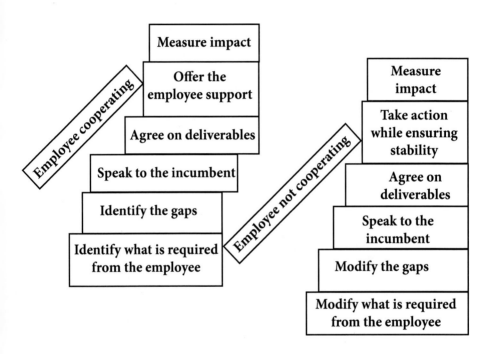

We must always remember that the most effective and at the same time the most productive resource any company has, is its people! This means that time and money must be spent on maintaining the organisational culture. It is important that employees are reasonably satisfied with their working conditions, remuneration, and management style. This can be achieved by ensuring that there is a clear transfer of information and a clear articulation of what is expected of the individual in relation to the organisational direction. It is important for managers to be decisive and not allow a challenge with an employee to spiral out of control.

There are many ways of rewarding employees for excellence, such as annual awards that only need the event and a certificate, yet generates huge excitement that the company recognises delivery. It is also important to mention good performing staff in public forums of the organisation.

5.   Values

In the work place, there are diverse personal values; yet there is an expectation of common values. As a CEO, don't let the values develop from the behaviour, habits, and practices of the employees, but consciously advocate fixed values. The organisational values should be concluded through a consultative process and not be focused on issues that have no relevance to the core mandate of the organisation. The values should reflect both tangible and non tangible issues.

- **Tangible**

Tangible values reflect issues relating to core business and there are several statements that can be used to represent the position of the company in this regard.

> **The customer is always right.**

> **This company adopted the triple bottom line: Profit, Environment and Social Responsibility**

> **This company abides by the King 3 principles on Good Governance**

- **Non tangible**

The non tangible values reflect the 'heart' of the organisation. Employees should be able to identify these values in their own lives and consider themselves part of the life of the organisation.

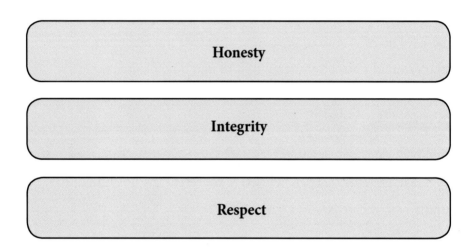

You need to reflect on your own values and assess the impact that your personal values will have within the company as the CEO. Your values should be in line with the organisational value and if not, it is your duty to review the company values or learn from them and add or change your own values. If you have not taken the time to consider values, please ensure that you reflect on what matters to you as an individual and also in your role as a CEO. The impact of adopting personal values and ensuring that the company you lead has values, allows clarity of mind to teach what you know and learn from others for the growth of the company and also for personal growth.

6.   The need for change

Being a new CEO, you will inevitably identify issues that you wish to change in the company to adapt it to your management style. Always remember that you are not necessarily changing because it is expected that you align the company to a path of sustainability. If you change for the sake of change to make your mark as the new CEO, this will backfire on you severely.

The first point of reference of what you need to change in the company would have emerged during the interview process with questions assessing your intention to create a more effective, efficient, cost-effective, and well-managed organisation. Furthermore, you will identify gaps and/or opportunities from the information you read about the organisation.

Your meeting with your management team members, both as a team and individuals will also inform you as to what needs to change. There will also be a need to evaluate the change you institute and where necessary, change the change.

The following process map shows the leads to change rather than just instituting change in a vacuum:

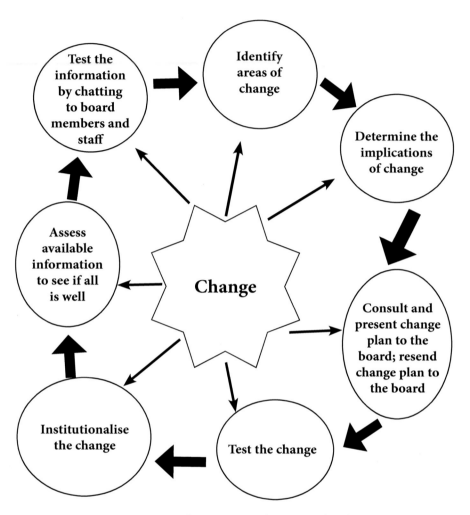

It is important to monitor change. It is also critical to know that in the event that your governing structure does not agree with your change or insists on guiding you with the issues that require change; it is your responsibility to follow the guidance within the rules of the organisation. It is not advisable to force your will as the change will be not supported and in turn not work. With the ever-changing world in this age of technology, you must be flexible and focus on what will maintain sound relationships to benefit the company rather than focusing on what you want to do.

7.   Putting a plan in place

As the head of administration (CEO), it is critical that you put a plan in place. There is a saying, 'If you fail to plan, you plan to fail.' There are countless organisations that are in crisis management mode, drawing management into micro managing operations rather than maintaining the organisation's future and big picture. The plan should be able to answer certain probing questions, namely,

- **What is the status quo?**

- **What is working?**

- **What is not working?**

- **What are the opportunities?**

- **What are the short-term, medium-term, and long-term interventions that need to be brought in?**

There are CEOs who are so obsessed with planning what can be achieved, that they neglect implementation, which displays what is being achieved. So when requested to present on delivery, the CEO expresses his vision for the future. Put simply, as the CEO, you must walk with your eyes seeing the target (vision), while walking confidently on the ground seizing opportunities that draw you closer to your destination.

Your plan as a CEO should also focus on reducing the temptation to manage crisis situations and focus on predicting what will impact the organisation's operations against the vision. The short-term planning should be annual and linked to available resources both financial and human. The bigger picture for the organisation should be conceptualised in five-year pockets and the long-term vision for a twenty-year period. The reason for the annual and five-year planning processes is to ensure that the changing environment can be factored into the long-term vision. The planning regime should be as described here:

- **Short-term planning**

The short-term plan should look at quick wins and opportunities against the budget. The plan should include the following:

- **Reflect on the vision**

- **Reflect on the past year**

- **Determine the priorities for the new year**

- **Explore the opportunities**

- **Confirm multiyear projects**

- **Reflect on controls and risks**

- **Medium-term planning**

The medium-term plan should be done every three to five years.

This planning process addresses the plans that are more of a capital nature and require a multiyear approach. In the case of a construction company, fleet and plant may constitute the medium-term plan and can therefore make these purchases on higher purchase. The medium-term agenda will include but not limited to the following:

- **Reflection on the vision**

- **Executive appointments**

- **Medium-term expenditure**

- **Governance review**

- **Confirmation or appointment of board members**

- **Investments**

- **Collaboration and partnerships**

- **Long-term planning**

The long-term issues require visionary thinking that looks at the crystal ball of the future potential of the organisation. This thinking is expected to rise above the day-to-day challenges that emerge.

- ✔ **Nature of business**

- ✔ **Marketing strategy and brand placement**

- ✔ **Supplier relationships**

- ✔ **Capital investments**

- ✔ **Review and extend customer base**

- ✔ **Assess product mix**

8.   Selling change to key stakeholders

When people in a company are accustomed to doing things in a particular manner for years, it becomes difficult for them to accept that change needs to be made because the changes impact individuals and their comfort zones established in the organisation.

It is important for you to make a list of all your stakeholders, followed by a categorisation from most relevant to potential stakeholder. The categorisation is intended to ensure that the flow of organisational information is carefully sifted to avoid exposure of valuable information. It is also necessary to deal with all stakeholders as though they are the most important.

There are internal and external stakeholders in every company and you as the CEO must select the relevance and benefit of each one and determine the extent of the relationship. Coming to change, all your stakeholders will be affected in one way or the other by the change that you introduce and therefore, it is your responsibility to champion the change.

The first place to start to sell your change agenda is with your internal stakeholders such as your board and the organisation's employees. The main reason for making this the starting point is that you can convert these two key internal stakeholders into believers and advocates of the change. They should not promote the change as your idea, but own the change in order for external stakeholders to believe that the change will be effective and implementable.

It is always necessary to discuss your change agenda with the chairperson of your board followed by its members before a formal sitting to consider your change. This is done to ensure that your motive and intentions are understood and more importantly for you to enjoy advice that could prove valuable to adjust your concept with ideas from the board members.

With regard to staff, you will require a workforce to implement the change and therefore it is important that they understand and believe that the change is both necessary and will add value to the organisation.

9.　Crafting the new direction

Your letter of appointment as the CEO marks the beginning of a journey and new leadership within the organisation. Even if your approach and management style are similar to those of the previous incumbent, it will not be the same because your style will be influenced by many variables such as your background, education, experiences, beliefs, and values. The new road should be carefully planned within the context of the opportunities for the company with your personal career path.

Let me use the analogy of a road trip with you as the driver to make the point of crafting a new direction for the organisation. In the vehicle, you will have various passengers with a range of responsibilities and you must know where you are going and how you expect to get there. It is also critical for you to ensure that the vehicle is in good order and the necessary instruments and warning signs are in working order.

In a company, you will have computers, systems, tools, and human resources that are used for the direction of the organisation. It is also important for the route to be clear and in the case of the organisation, the vision is the route. The following diagram explains the route map.

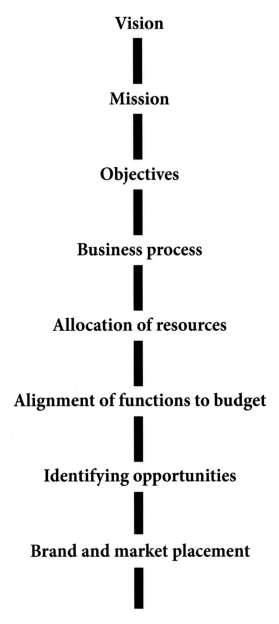

Vision

Mission

Objectives

Business process

Allocation of resources

Alignment of functions to budget

Identifying opportunities

Brand and market placement

The plans and vision for the future must be understood in the context of what can be achieved and also what the reality will be. What I mean is that your plans will not work out perfectly as planned and you must be able to assess what has worked and what needs to be changed.

10. Benchmarking

If you don't assess what is happening in your sector, you may have the false impression that you are doing well. There are countless companies with great products that have fallen short due to them being over confident and not reading the customer needs. It can also be said that the confidence of the individual functionaries within the company to prove their worth leads to them losing sight of shortcomings that could be a distraction from the main focus. There are critical areas that need to be considered when benchmarking as displayed in the diagram;

Remember though not to run your company by looking through the window all day to check what the neighbour is doing. Benchmarking should be built into the overall strategy and timed appropriately to allow maximum benefit.

Internal Considerations

✔   **What is their value proposition?**

✔   **Why will or why do people buy your products?**

✔   **What is the benefit of your product?**

✔   **Who is the client?**

Looking at the competition

✔   **What is their value proposition?**

✔   **What is the difference in the product mix between the organisations?**

✔   **What makes the opposition's products sell?**

✔   **Who is the client?**

Benchmark results

✔   **Confirm or refine value proposition**

✔   **Determine the product mix**

✔   **Marketing strategy adjusted**

✔   **Determine the new client profile**

11.   Pick your fights

Executive managers are faced with many decisions in any single day and therefore must have the strategic knowhow to assess the impact and/or value of every decision to determine the time and importance it is given. There is the old saying that, 'You may win this fight yet loose the war.' The sponsors, authors, or lobbyist of a decision will market the proposal in a manner that seeks to force the manager to think that the company will benefit from the decision. It is important for executives to, within seconds and in their mind, assess the required decision using the following probing questions:

- **Why is the decision necessary?**

- **Is the decision operational or strategic and does it fall within the scope of delegations?**

- **Who is the appropriate manager to make the decision?**

- **What are the financial implications?**

- **What are the risks?**

- **What are the opportunities?**

- **Is the sponsor of the decision the relevant colleague to present the proposal?**

- **Who will benefit from the decision and why?**

- **Will the decision contribute to core business?**

The probing questions will result in a firm conclusion whether you are the correct person to make the decision. If you are a control freak, you may want to make every decision and micro manage your colleagues, but rest assured that they will not grow and will let you down when it really matters as you do not give them an opportunity to take responsibility. A good executive manager will focus only on the issues that advance the growth, sustainability, and person of the organisation.

There are also many managers who thrive on the adrenalin rush of crisis. I was sitting in a top management meeting and a presentation was made by one of the middle managers of the company and he used the following words to lobby his proposal for a decision, 'Crisis – urgent – I am concerned – seriousness – implications – devastating effect... '. When a colleague uses such negativity, the intention is to transfer such to you, changing the very reason for you to make a decision from it being the right thing to do for the company to being the only thing to do! Always remember that such negativity is not always informed by a clear mind having taken every aspect into account, but by other factors including personal circumstances, emotional state of mind at the time, health, and feelings towards the company against the colleague's own place. It is only an ambulance or fire service that should invoke panic for fast decisions. This does not mean that decision should not be made due to urgent conditions within the organisation; however, such decisions must be informed, a clear mind having analysed all options using the earlier questions. So pick your fights and when you do, stand by your decision.

12.   Sustainability plan

Start with the end in mind! It is critical to know what will make your company become an institution or household brand name. There are products in the marketplace that become known for particular characteristics that appeal to a particular customer. For example, German car manufacturers have established themselves and their country to be associated with luxury cars, while Italy and its manufacturers are well known for super cars. My point is that branding of why your product is the best and basing that assumption on actual facts is the key to sustainability. If you take the example of a government department in any country, the marketing strategy cannot be a fast, efficient service because by nature, government is not fast and efficient due to the legitimate need for due process. Now due process allows government to produce a result that is intended to be fair, transparent, and equitable. This therefore means that an approach to marketing should reflect the public's ability to rely on the basic principles of fairness; this becomes the value proposition that sets the stage for sustainability.

If you recall the 2010 soccer world cup, many individuals and organisations established and or increased their businesses by investing huge amounts with the intention that the six-week event will result in a long-term benefit. After the last team left South Africa, many of these individuals and organisations folded as they were not sustainable. Sustainability should not be an emotional decision based on what is current. It is important to use a third party to assess the investment decisions for sustainability rather than relying on your gut feel. Okay, I agree that there should be a level of gut feel in all decisions. Successful businesses are not invested by people who think conventionally but by people who are willing to take a risk and follow their gut feel.

So, the sustainability plan should be constantly evaluated and gradually accepted that what works today may not work tomorrow. Sustainability is a strategic decision and not a nicety to have.

g. Operations

It is the detail that drives the strategy

1. Roles and responsibilities

Organisational structures are populated with functionaries and it is critical that the roles and responsibilities are clearly defined to avoid confusion. It is important for you as the CEO to understand your role as I have on many occasions witnessed heads of a companies trying to do everything by themselves. You may get it right by doing it yourself, but then not able to sustain the result. Your primary objective as CEO is to coordinate functions into the core business.

There can only be one CEO and if you are not the CEO don't assume the responsibilities of the CEO. It is also important that even though you may not consider the CEO competent, you respect the leadership. There are issues that you as an executive will have control over and there are issues that you have no control over – in this instance, the appointment of your supervisor is beyond your control and the type of character selected is also beyond your control. I hope all this is making sense – what I am saying is that, you must understand your role and focus on your outputs and responsibilities and not focus on what you may consider as short comings in your supervisor.

It is useful to hold an opinion on issues and voice that opinion, but be mindful of who is required to make the final decision and respect their role. Many decisions are lost because the person making the choice is not relevant. There is also a growing tendency for managers to sign 'pp' on behalf of the executive opening up the company to abuse where employees could commit the company materially.

Furthermore, as an executive you will be expected to be involved in micro decisions that seem urgent, yet have no direct benefit to the organisation. You should guard against someone else's urgent matter becoming your urgent matter. You can offer guidance, but refrain from being involved as you will not be able to see it through if something goes wrong later. I say this also in the light of knowing that there are employees who choose to involve the most senior official in order to avoid taking responsibility.

As the CEO, it is also important that you allow your staff to fulfil their role and make decisions. Do not be a control freak and want to know everything and decide on everything. On the dashboard of a car, there are only a few functions that offer you peace of mind that all is functioning well – in the same manner you should have a dashboard of what matters to you in your organisation. In other words, 'pick your fights'. You should know what the implications are of all issues within the company and then know which ones are important and which should be important to someone else; or else you will be caught up trying to do everything.

Please refrain from being a CEO who wants the role but not the responsibility. It is not easy to be an executive and you must be able to think above the daily problems and navigate solutions that will build you and the organisation.

2.   Output

The output in a supermarket is the checkout where customers pay even though other functions are important such as packing in the stores. However, if all the staff were to assist with packing in the back of the store, the customers would not be able to pay for their goods and without an income there would be no store to pack. As the CEO, ensure that all your employees know and understand what the organisation's output is and what their role is towards the deliverables. There is the story told of the cleaner at the American space station who was asked, 'So what is your role here?' The response was swift and confident, 'I am assisting to send people into space.' It is this understanding of the deliverables that makes a company stand apart from the rest.

You must align your team to be focused on your core business in order to enjoy the maximum benefit from the existing potential. The following diagram shows the typical process flow within an organisation:

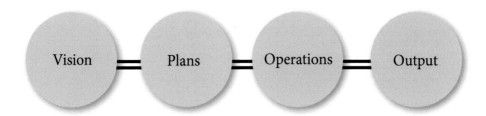

Every company must have a drawing board where plans are crafted based on the vision and desired outputs. The quality of the outputs adjusts the vision. Your main focus as a CEO should be on the operations that generate results while using the vision as a guide and path. Everything you do has an output and everything you don't do has an output, which is nothing. Yes, nothing is also a result, an output. What you put in is what you will get out.

3. Conflict management

Conflict arises in the workplace primarily due to lack of communication. One of the key ingredients for conflict is to leave matters unresolved. It is important that a common approach is adopted and documented on the guiding principles of conflict resolution. The obvious drivers of conflict should be clear to you as a manager and you need to minimise the risk in those areas through consultation. The methods employed to manage conflict should be negotiated and agreed to by all. You will find it more effective to address conflict between individuals in the workplace when there is an overall conflict resolution guide in place.

There are employees in every environment who thrive on drama and consider negative energy or action in the workplace as being productive to the extent that their days are consumed by discussions about who should be removed. In most cases, the bearer of the conversation is usually someone who has no right, power, or authority to do something and who is frustrated by that very fact.

Also note that employees have expectations on you as the CEO regarding how you will address them and the issue that they are raising; therefore, always be mindful that you could upset or even offend a colleague without even realising it. Always qualify your actions and be very clear on why you are taking a certain direction rather than having the opinion that you are in charge and everyone must do as you say. Yes they will do as you say today but build up a destructive path for you tomorrow.

I always say that an argument does not produce a winner, both parties loose. A conflict is in most part a miscommunication between two people. As the CEO, you must apply reason and logic to your management style in order to avoid conflict.

Apart from internal conflict, you must ensure that there is a constant exchange of ideas between you and your stakeholders. Communication will result in all parties knowing what to expect from each other. Word of mouth remains the most convincing sales method and you don't want the message to your stakeholders to be a bad encounter by a customer.

4.   Bad days test the emotions

There is no perfect life and in the professional world you will experience bad days that will test your emotions to the point that you will ask yourself whether it is worth it to carry on or be part of the madness. Your emotions will be tested in various ways and it is important to keep your focus. Don't allow your emotions to rule your response to situations that emerge. Never draw conclusions on why people behave in a particular manner and first try to understand negativity rather than using assumptions. Recently, I attended a meeting in which I was the most senior person; however, the chairperson treated me with contempt. At first I wanted to address his behaviour, but rather chose to observe and tolerate the abuse. I left the meeting without having the opportunity to state my purpose for being in the meeting. Later that day I was informed that the same chairperson had resigned from his job just before the meeting; hence his behaviour. I know what you are thinking, that he still did not have the right to be rude – I agree. However, all behaviour has context.

When you are having a bad day, limit your communication with colleagues to avoid emotional bursts that may not be able to be withdrawn. There is a growing focus on the concept of emotional intelligence, which speaks to making your reaction humorous towards your surroundings. At any one time in your working day as the CEO, you could be answering two phones, writing an email, preparing for a meeting, talking to people who need your time, and handle many other issues at the same time. I have not even mentioned the personal challenges that you may need to address while dealing with the work challenges. This complex environment that executives are expected to work in nowadays leads to high stress levels and a dominance of negative emotions that are aimed at trying to survive. In days gone by, exchange of information took time due to the limited communication available and therefore, you would have sufficient time to think through a response to a problem before responding. However, with technology, the problem comes direct to your cellular phone and prompts a response immediately.

You must process information in your mind using the robot colour scheme of green for problem, amber for urgent problem, and red for critical problem.

5. Communication

Success or failure of a company can be determined by perception; therefore, perception needs to be managed effectively using a communication strategy. Communication needs to be directed at two distinct stakeholders, namely, internal and external. The message to the two stakeholder groups will be different based on the issue that needs to be communicated.

5.1 Internal stakeholders

Information and communication are also packaged for the internal stakeholders based on what would be relevant. There are confidential issues and also issues of intellectual property that need to be best-kept secrets because the implications of this information leaking or being known would negatively impact the organisation. There are a range of internal stakeholders, namely,

✔   **Trade unions**

✔   **Management**

✔   **Other organised formations such as youth and women's groups**

✔   **Communications department is applicable**

5.2   External stakeholders

Every organisation has its own unique set of stakeholders. You must categorise your stakeholders in order to have a predictable relationship that dictates the nature of the relationship, value, and time required of the relationship. Typically, your stakeholders from outside will be made up of the following broad areas:

✔   **Customers**

✔   **Service providers**

✔   **Other companies**

✔   **Research institutions**

✔   **Marketing companies**

✔   **Media**

The key to a successful organisation is to know what to communicate, to whom, and why. Communication reduces the element of perception and maintains the focus on the real issues rather than introducing speculation.

6.   Risk

All organisations carry a risk profile. There are several risk areas including financial risk that normally comes out of the biggest. The focus should not be only on the immediate risks, but also on the more long-term risks that are considerably more devastating than the immediate issues. The risks should be categorised as there are both positive and negative risks.

✔   **Positive risks**

This primarily relates to the risk appetite of the company and what it is prepared to do to achieve its objectives. You must be willing to take risks as a CEO that will advance your organisation's progress. The risks should be limited only to the short term as this can be contained, should it not work. Any long-term risks should be at the board level; however, such risks should be low. Risks should be determined and tabled to the board as described in the following sample:

Risk item	Low risk	Medium risk	High risk
Financial: cash flow is a major challenge			
Disciplinary measures against non-performance			
Leasing of vehicles may be impacted on through the interest rate			
Competition may invent new products			

✔ **Negative risks**

The table above is also relevant to negative risks. Some of the negative risks are theft and change in market conditions. The CEO must prepare a risk register and have a dashboard showing the most significant risks in the main functional areas as displayed here.

Low risk	Medium risk	High risk
Finances	Staff	Supply chain
Market	Board	Perception

The risks will differ from organisation to organisation and it may be necessary, funds permitting, to request an independent person to do the assessment as the risks reflected should inform strategy and focus in the next year. The greatest risk to any organisation remains its people and there should be constant communication of what is expected of staff and what is the benefit of the expectation.

7.   Institutional knowledge

Every activity of everyday in an organisation is a collection of
knowledge on how to do things or how not to do things. So, it reflects
success or lessons. It is crucial to maintain a resource bank that can
store information and allow the organisation to look ahead with a clear
picture of what's behind. There are many types of knowledge and every
type holds a different value based on who is giving and who requires
the information. Some organisations over emphasize on certain
information, which may not hold a material advantage; however, it is
close to the heart of the CEO or board. This scenario is acceptable on
condition that it is clearly understood why the information is being
considered as critical rather than motivating its importance based on
personal feeling.

As the CEO, it is your role to protect the organisation's knowledge
and also ensure that the acquired knowledge is not the copyright
of another organisation. Also place a value on information and sell
such information in order to generate income as if you don't do this;
someone else will package the information differently and steal it
anyway. The most significant knowledge that your organisation has is
its resolutions.

8.   Controls

Shrinkage in an organisation can lead to its fall. As the CEO, you must prepare systems and controls that ensure the effective and efficient utilisation of resources. However, you must ensure that controls do not impede your organisation from progress. You must place basic control measures in place including the use of resources such as vehicles and equipment that carry high value and can serve as a high cost to the organisation. You should also ensure that there are strict controls in your supply chain. In order to affect controls, you must determine delegations and decision making that includes the value of purchases and responsibility to allocate assets.

The approach to controls must be within the context of the following questions:

- **What do I need to do to protect the assets of the organisation?**

- **How will I handle theft and abuse?**

- **How do I implement controls while ensuring that this does not interfere with the progress and opportunities the organisation has?**
- **Who should be responsible for which controls?**

It is important to use the control framework to guide operations. The board will look at the strategic controls, such as who signs on the bank accounts and enters into contracts and makes big decisions. Management should ensure that all operational controls are in place.

9. Understanding the production line through project management

You must know what makes your end product – what are the functions and processes that lead to the product or service that you offer. There should be a standard format of production. With the complex nature of doing business in the modern day, the concept of project management becomes critical for all functions within the company. For example, in the past, the human resource function was solely there in a company for recruitment; however, within the new dynamics of how business works, the human resources function now must include employee wellness, industrial relations, labour forums, and a range of other functions that impact directly on productivity.

Over the past twenty years, the project management concept has become increasingly popular allowing managers to become more flexible in understanding all aspects of the business. What I mean is that you must know every part of the business. There is a project cycle in most activities in a company that require project management approach. The following diagram displays a typical project management cycle:

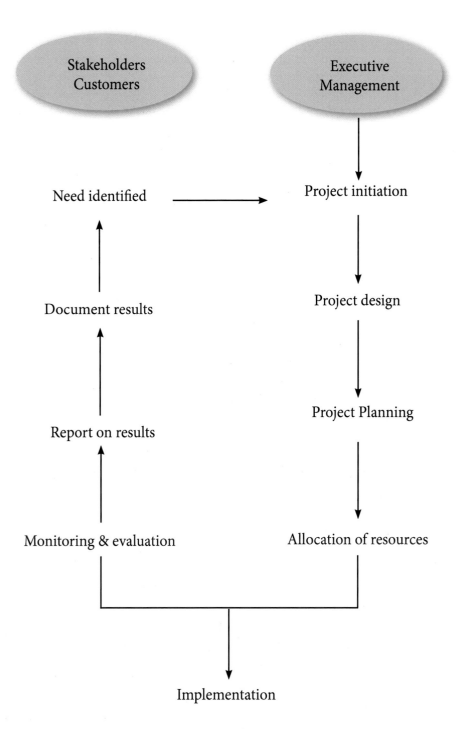

10. Innovation

Every day there are new ideas born that pose a threat to your company and its focus. You must dedicate some time to innovation to keep the company relevant to the growing technology and market forces. Your innovation should consider the following questions:

✔   **Will the company advance from the innovation?**

✔   **Will it add value to productivity?**

✔   **Will employees be better off and be more motivated?**

Innovation can also come from your employees in the most unexpected way if they are allowed space to be creative. I have an uncle who moved to Canada on a work permit as a boilermaker. During the construction of a pipeline, there was a difficult bend that needed to be navigated and the technical experts insisted that only a company from Italy could develop the tool to ensure that the task was completed. My uncle who was not highly placed in the company and also not permanently employed due to his citizenship, overheard the conversation and requested an audience to share his experience and knowledge in resolving the challenge. The short end of the story is that he fabricated a manual device and saved the company millions of dollars.

On the other extreme, there are people who just lack creativity and their companies don't allow space for innovation by putting rules that are impossible to break even for the advancement of creativity. One such case is a joke made about municipal workers. A man walked past a municipal worker digging holes in an orderly fashion and a little behind this worker was another municipal worker filling the holes will soil. The passer by stopped in amazement and asked the man filling the holes, 'Sir, why is he digging holes and why are you filling the same holes? Is this not unnecessary and wasteful?' The reply was swift from the breathless worker, 'Yes, we are both so frustrated as there is a guy who plants a tree after my colleague has dug the hole and I close the hole with the tree in – but he is sick today!' The bewildered bystander continued, 'Why don't you just plant the tree first then close the hole?' The employee seemed irritated and responded, 'Sir, my job description says that I close the holes not plant trees, I am not prepared to do someone else's job.' This is also true of many private companies who put rules in place that compromise common sense.

Create the environment in your company to reward innovation and allow your employees to explore new ideas, obviously not at the expense of production. The creative mind should be within the normal cause of doing business.

11. Decision making

Executive management is expected to make decisions. A decision taken in the best interest of the organisation, but turns out to be a wrong decision will still not impact as negatively as a no decision. I have witnessed a growing trend of what I will call 'the democratisation of administration' – by this I am talking about the obsession with meetings to create joint ownership of decisions. Now if you are a CEO and have delegated powers and functions from your governing structure, you are expected to make decisions within your scope. There are executives that consider the risk and implications of decisions and then refuse to make the decision and bring it to a management meeting for a collective decision so that if it does not work out they can refer to the minutes of the meeting as proof that it was not their decision and they were the executing authority of a collective decision. This is poor management and executives should not rely on collective body for operational decisions. Any decision made in the best interest of the company and within your scope of authority to decide that turns out to be wrong will be more than likely supported and rectified. However, a 'no decision' policy on your part is much more damning to the company than the wrong decision. You are an executive with the power to make decisions.

In the decision-making process, you must separate the range of decisions that need to be taken and place them into categories in order for the appropriate functionary to make the decision. The following diagram shows the decision-making scope of each of the functional areas in a typical organisation:

Governance structure	Executive Management	Operational Management
Approval of the budget	Provide secretarial support to the board	Align productivity and business processes to budget and business plan
Appoint Executives	Implement board resolutions	Implement core business
Approve contracts	Appoint operational staff	Deal with customers and service providers
Enter into binding agreements	Aligned approved budget to operations	Address complaints
Make investments	Prepare business plan	Manage daily office activities
Approve the brand strategy	Manage the day-to-day activities of the company	Manage the logistical movements of the employees
Give guidance to administration through resolutions		

SUPPORT STAFF

Just to end this section – your company must have a decision-making process that includes authorisation levels and approval processes. For example, if a letter needs to be written to your board chairperson, your secretary will not be the signatory to the letter but yourself. The manner in which decisions are made makes or breaks an organisation.

12.   The moment

One of my mentors made a profound statement in my view that resonates with me when the going gets tough. He said, 'It took me fifteen years to become an overnight success.' Success is a journey not a destination, but along the way you must be able to identify key success factors that you can consider as milestones, which bring the dream closer. What does it matter to cry if no one can comfort you? What does it matter if we are excited if there is no one to share the excitement? When your company celebrates success it should be institutional more than personal. You built up through strategy, management style, and operational efficiencies all for the moment when it all comes together.

Talking about coming together, have you ever done a puzzle, say a thousand pieces? It may take you awhile, but in the end you can complete it. Now the most significant moment is when you place the last piece to complete the puzzle. Suddenly, in that moment, the struggle of separating the pieces into colours and similar shades and putting them together becomes worth the effort. There are people who give up before completing the task and offer pages and pages of excuses or should I say reasons for stopping. Yet the main reason was that the focus had changed. To reach that 'moment' in the company, there must be total dedication to the conclusion of the task. Let me place this in poetry.

The Moment

The excitement of the dream, the determination of the mind to see the
vision
Thoughts of opportunities dominate the fragile brain that can be swayed
A plan is designed with options filtered and refined
I am on my way and the moment I will attain
One step into the route to the dream and the cold of the dew confront
what I thought I could do

Should I step back into the comfort of the ideal or do I step forward
towards the prize
An audience I have and critics confirm that my doubt is about the
unreachable
Because no one around victory has found, my step is unknown and the
dream but a frown
With no one on my side, my cold steps are loud
The pain in my veins I sacrifice for gain

There are times when I want to stop and rather watch the few who dare to
be true to their dream
A lonely voice lifts me up and confirms that I can pass.
With the last step in sight the moment arrives

From the lonely journey the critics are back and offer their support to the
victory knowing that their negativity is history

The road's been too tough to fight and the moment too precious to dilute
The moment has arrived, the moment has come
Cometh the moment cometh the man!

h. Who Can Be a CEO?

Don't be limited by what you think you can't do as you may just be able to do it if others consider you able.

There are key attributes that constitute the character of a CEO and these can be divided into two distinct areas, namely, personal and professional. The list below shows that there is no perfect CEO and there are many factors that contribute to the success or failure of a CEO. The list of attributes is not limited to the ones mentioned and will vary from person to person based on the type of job. I will not go into detail in this area, but rather intend raising your awareness that you are first a human being before you are a functionary.

1.1   Attitude

It is said that 70 percent of a CEO's qualification to be a good CEO is the attitude and the remaining 30 percent allocated to skill, experience, and education. Your attitude should include understanding people and approaching every situation with respect, calmness, and rational thinking. Yes, you are the boss and no one will take that position away from you except your board. So there is no reason to prove it to those around you. Avoid being a bully as management by fear results in you being managed by your colleagues and not feared. You will be set up and will not enjoy loyalty and support.

A good CEO is one who is able to explain and communicate decisions even if there is no agreement. Also avoid using your position to institute protocol that gives you the false sense of importance. It is the position that is important and not you in the context of the job.

1.2   Ambition

There is nothing wrong with being ambitious, but don't go through your life doing whatever it takes to make it to the next level. Your ambitions must also be mindful of the fact that you should grow incrementally. The challenge with ambition is that you may consider yourself much more competent than your supervisor based on your ambition; however, you must know your place. To take this further, as the CEO you should only speak when spoken to in the board meeting rather than attempting to impress your board that you are intelligent. You don't have to impress them; that is one of the main reasons why they appointed you and therefore know that you are clever.

1.3   Beliefs

I once transported three school principals between two towns after a workshop that I was facilitating. As we approached the destination, we witnessed a number of police vehicles persuing a taxi on a corrugated road. Given the speed at which he was travelling, the driver of the taxi had no intention of stopping, while on the other hand, the police seemed to be confident that the pursuit would end with them stopping the taxi.

One of my passengers expressed her disgust at what she was seeing. It was my assumption that her reaction was related to the fact that the taxi was fleeing from the police and should stop. To my absolute surprise, this community leader and educator of future leaders and responsible citizens explained, 'Why don't the police leave the poor man alone? Don't they have anything better to do for themselves than to chase a man trying to earn a living?' This was obviously how the educator viewed life and these were the beliefs she held.

1.4   Choices

In all that we do, we make choices and the multiplication of the choices establishes our path. The choices we make are informed and influenced by our emotional state, mood, preferences, context, environment, and many other factors at that point in time.

Every choice has a responsibility and consequence – we are required to analyse the level of risk involved and/or benefit from the choice and make the choice. Now, before you think this is some idealistic proposal, we don't realise how fast our brains work to make a number of choices in a short space of time.

Do you realise that when we greet someone, we have made a choice that is informed by possible benefit and when we choose not to greet someone, we have made a choice of the consequences associated with generally accepted behaviour by human beings. This is said in the context that the reference is to the greeting of someone we know or someone we wish to know and/or even someone who wishes to know us.

1.5   Compassion

Be mindful that there are people who require your help in various ways in the same manner that you require other people's help. I have heard people say that they have no sympathy for the beggar on the street corner because the beggar should look for a real job. My response is always to explain that standing on your feet the whole day begging is a job that is more difficult than most.

It is important to treat all people with respect and not attempt to remove their dignity that is not yours to take, but rather encourage people to be more than they can be.

1.6   Emotional intelligence

There are many things that happen in a day that make us happy and many that make us sad. Some days are good, others are great, while you will have bad days and terrible days. Don't transfer your negative energy if you are in a bad mood and expect others to understand or sympathise. You must be in control of your emotions at all times.

Remember also that the issues that matter to you may not matter to those around you. However, if the issues that matter to you are of material interest to your company, share your focus on the issue with colleagues in order to enjoy their support because they understand why it is a priority. You should also ensure that how you feel does not impact on the decisions you need to make. Your decisions should be focused and based on real issues and not on your feelings.

1.7   Education

Ensure that you hold the necessary qualifications and continue to grow your understanding of your surroundings. Be educated, educate, and continue to seek education. You must seek education using the following approach;

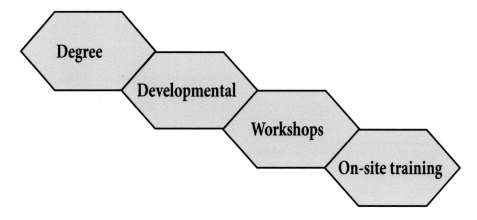

1.8   Fun

There should be an element of fun in you and you should not be ridged that life is serious enough for you to walk around with a concerned look on your face all the time. Don't be a workaholic and ensure that you allocate time for other critical areas of your life including fun.

I hope that you don't consider watching television as fun – it is not interactive and does not stimulate your soft side to consider tangible issues within the context of who you are. I am not suggesting that you become Trevor Noah in your office, but make provision to contextualise everything in order to produce a balance, which must include the lighter side of life.

1.9   Grasp of logic and reason

Due to the complex nature of business, sometimes common sense is not so common. You must apply common sense when making decisions. Ensure that you have a clear grasp of logic; however, don't rely only on logic in multi-dimensional professional challenges. On the other hand, you have heard people say, 'Please be reasonable.' The definition of what constitutes being reasonable differs from person to person and from issue to issue. Yes, be reasonable, but don't dilute the facts and hard decisions with this approach.

1.10   Health

As the CEO, you should not neglect your health but constantly assess the pressure on you. Everyone will want their pound of flesh from you, but choose your fights and create a focus – as for the rest, 'smile and wave'. If you work yourself to death, you will be remembered for the time before your funeral and thereafter – the show must go on. Recently, I was approached by the husband of a colleague who made the following statement, 'Sir, I don't want my wife to be overworked because if she dies you will immediately appoint someone else to act in her position to carry out her duties, while I will have to mourn her passing for the rest of my life.' Well, this statement is true, but some people use this approach to justify sheer laziness and a lack of commitment.

It is also important to eat right. I weighed 134 kilograms at some point and could feel that I was unhealthy and could end up with a stroke – a heart attack. I decided to lose weight and lost 46 kilograms and maintained an active gym routine. You may say that you don't have the time – make the time or you will run out of time. I also suggest that you see a psychologist from time to time just to chat about how you feel – the conversation allows you to think about things from different contexts and allows you the opportunity to focus on what you need to do.

1.11 People

You exist alongside the existence of other people and you need those around you as much as they need you. There are groups of people that should matter in your life, namely:

✔ **Family**

✔ **Community**

✔ **Colleagues**

✔ **People at your place of worship**

You must establish relationships that will work for you and the only way to do this is to work on your relationships. Those around you should not feel that you are using them but rather consider you an asset to their own needs in their existence.

1.12 Travel

You must travel as this is one of the most effective ways of gaining passive knowledge that becomes embedded in who you are. Travel also allows you to remove yourself from the issues that drive you to focus on the small issues and gives you a window to see the bigger picture.

Encourage your colleagues to travel as well, so that they can gain a broader perspective on issues in order to become more productive in their dealings with you.

1.13   Values

How you conduct yourself reflects the values by which you live. It becomes critical to assess what your values are and continue to sharpen your behaviour to reflect these values. Your values could include the following, but may not be limited to:

✔   **Honesty**

✔   **Integrity**

✔   **Compassion**

✔   **Building relationships**

Concluding remarks

An ordinary human being can do extraordinary things, which in turn makes them become experts, leaders, and wise. You must do what you do consistently without compromise. Obviously, you will make mistakes and learn lessons – then you can fix your walk and confidently walk tall. You can do it!!!

GASTER SHARPLEY

i. Key Success Factors of a CEO

Networking contributes to net worth

1. Networking

As the CEO, your stakeholders will expect you to be available and relevant to their expectations. You must know your stakeholders and focus on keeping them interested in your company. Reinvent yourself and ensure that you are able to make the products and services relevant. Networking takes time and may not show immediate results, but you must build up a relationship that will see you enjoy full benefit. This can be achieved by being trustworthy and committed to the issues that matter to the stakeholders.

2. Manage perception by keeping the focus on the big picture

Know what you want to achieve and work on it all the time even when people may consider you a failure or a lost cause. Perception makes or breaks a company. You must believe in what you do and ensure that your colleagues also believe in it because if there is doubt, everyone will not take the business serious.

3. Establish a team

You cannot work alone and must establish a team. Just be careful not to mislead your colleagues to thinking that you are all equal in the workplace. Let me explain, you are all equal in the eyes of the law and the Almighty Lord; however, every functionary in the workplace has different responsibilities, roles, and positions. So, the team is in line with the job description, which makes you able to function, and all the various functions create the productivity required for a successful company.

4. See and seize opportunities

Opportunities present themselves daily to businesses and as the top executive you must see and seize these opportunities. Avoid being opportunistic but seek out opportunities. I believe that the difference between seeking out opportunities and being an opportunist is your ability to see an opportunity through helping someone or another company with a challenge they have. Being an opportunist is seeing the weaknesses in others and wanting to take advantage of this to your benefit – the benefit will however be short-lived.

5. Basic advice on networking

DO'S

- Celebrate the success of others

- Know your product

- Follow up

- Be humble

- It is pointless to prove a point

- Empower others by sharing ideas

DON'TS

- Don't lie

- Don't name drop

- Don't undermine others

- Don't work as an island

The Executive Manager in Me

I walk with confidence knowing that my heart is clean of all greed, anger, and petty strife.

I am an executive who understands the dynamics and complexities of the company and is not moved by sensationalism that lingers daily to fulfil the egos of the opportunist who wants my position, its benefits, and authority but never its sacrifices and responsibility.

I must enjoy what I do because I do what I enjoy.

I must understand those around me and play the rich diversity to the benefit of the productivity.

I must know my place and place into perspective what I know as what I know should be in context of what others wish to know.

Building a team is not for compromise and common vision is certain.

Making the team rich with shared ideas and collective wisdom to build the company must be my drive to keep it all alive.

I will not interpret confidence with competence and seek to support the focused colleagues who know which battles need to be fought.

I can't do everything and must choose some things because if I do everything I will lose the value in some things and get nothing done.

I won't always get it right, but focussing on the right may destract from focussing on the outcome which may result in productive right.

There will be times when I need to change my mind, times when I need to admit to being wrong, times when the pressure is beyond measure.

Let those times fall on a foundation of trust and support knowing that the basics are in place.

GASTER SHARPLEY

The proceeds of this book to be donated to:

PEGGY NESTA FOUNDATION
P O BOX 13330, Vincent, 5217
Tel.: 043 727 1070
Registration number: 2011/004481/08
Bank Details:
Nedbank, Branch Code: 10142100
Account Number: 1010522175